**Rookie
Get Ready
to Code**™

Design
a Game

Marcie Flinchum Atkins

Content Consultant

Sarah Otts
Scratch Online Community Developer
MIT Media Lab, Massachusetts Institute of Technology

Reading Consultant

Jeanne M. Clidas, Ph.D.
Reading Specialist

Children's Press®
An Imprint of Scholastic Inc.

Library of Congress Cataloging-in-Publication Data
Names: Atkins, Marcie Flinchum, author.
Title: Design a game/by Marcie Flinchum Atkins.
Description: New York, NY: Children's Press, an imprint of Scholastic Inc., 2019. |
Series: Rookie get ready to code | Includes index.
Identifiers: LCCN 2018028369| ISBN 9780531132272 (library binding) | ISBN 9780531137024 (paperback)
Subjects: LCSH: Computer games—Design—Juvenile literature. | Computer games—Programming—Juvenile
literature.
Classification: LCC QA76.76.C672 A89 2019 | DDC 794.8/1525—dc23

Produced by Spooky Cheetah Press
Creative Direction: Judith E. Christ for Scholastic Inc.
Design: Brenda Jackson

Published in 2019 by Children's Press, an imprint of Scholastic Inc.

Printed in North Mankato, MN, USA 113

SCHOLASTIC, CHILDREN'S PRESS, GET READY TO CODE™, and associated logos are trademarks and/or
registered trademarks of Scholastic Inc.

1 2 3 4 5 6 7 8 9 10 R 28 27 26 25 24 23 22 21 20 19

Scholastic Inc., 557 Broadway, New York, NY 10012.

Photos ©: cover: baona/iStockphoto; cover background: RioAbajoRio/Shutterstock; cover and throughout:
the8monkey/iStockphoto; inside cover and throughout: pmmix/Shutterstock; 4: dmitriylo/Shutterstock;
5: Bianca Alexis Photography; 7: Oleksiy Maksymenko Photography/Alamy Images; 8: Alamy Images;
9: tuthelens/Shutterstock; 9 inset screen: Alamy Images; 11 top: Kevin Britland/Alamy Images; 11 center:
Andrey_Popov/Shutterstock; 11 bottom: incamerastock/Alamy Images; 13 center: Andersen Ross/Getty
Images; 13 bottom left: pressureUA/iStockphoto; 13 bottom right: veryan dale/Alamy Images; 14-15 cubic
characters: kmls/Shutterstock; 14 street: pixeldreams.eu/Shutterstock; 14-15 logs: anna_wizard/Shutterstock;
15 axe: non157 pixel art/Shutterstock; 15 hammer: kozheko/Shutterstock; 17: Ian Dagnall/Alamy Images;
19: The Asahi Shimbun/Getty Images; 21: carl michelle/Alamy Images; 23: Ibusca/iStockphoto;
25: Destina156/Dreamstime; 27: Rob Monk/Edge Magazine/Getty Images; 28 bear: abramsdesign/
Shutterstock; 28 paper: Zoia Lukianova/Dreamstime; 30 super mario: marysuperstudio/
Shutterstock; 30 coin: La Gorda/Shutterstock.

TABLE OF CONTENTS

Chapter 1

The World of Video Games

Do you love video games? Have you ever wondered how they are made? The first thing game designers do is create a world. They create characters and a story. They think about what could happen in the game. Then they create a **storyboard**. That outlines all the possible actions in the game.

storyboard

The world the designers create depends on the type of game.

Tetris is a strategy game. Strategy games make the player think through moves in order to win.

In racing games, the player drives a vehicle to the finish line.

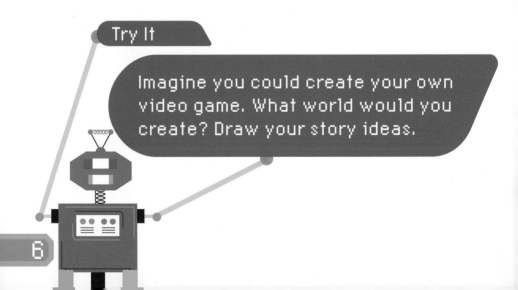

Try It

Imagine you could create your own video game. What world would you create? Draw your story ideas.

You can play *Tetris* on your phone.

Adventure games allow you to role-play. You can pretend to be a character.

Super Mario Bros. is a platformer game. Players earn points by escaping enemies and jumping around obstacles.

character

Random obstacles
and rewards help make
a game exciting.

Different games are designed for different devices. Arcade games are big machines. You have to pay each time you play. Video game consoles let you play games at home on a TV. A handheld device plays games formatted for a smaller screen, like the one on a phone or tablet. Players who are connected to the Internet can play against others anywhere in the world!

What is your favorite way to play?

arcade
game

video
game
console

handheld
device

11

Chapter 2

Controlling the Action

After the type of game is chosen, **programmers** get to work. Programmers write the code for the computer. Codes are specific directions for the computer to follow. Programmers write code for all the possible actions for a character.

For example, arrows on a keyboard or controller make the character move. When an arrow is pushed, the character goes left, right, up, or down.

Controlling Devices

controller

These are all different ways to control a character.

touch screen

Games

keyboard

An **algorithm** is a set of steps that makes an action happen.

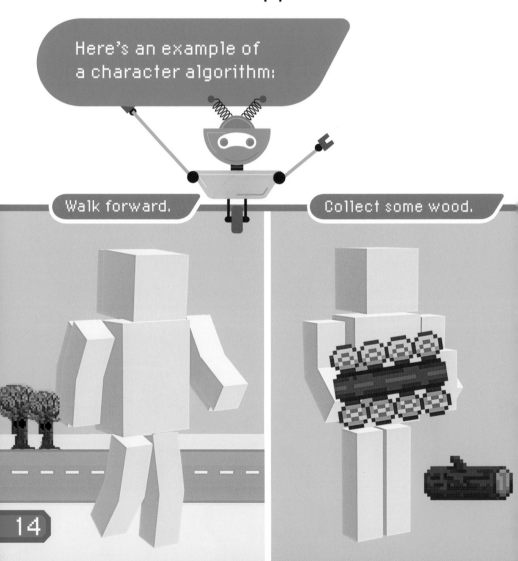

Here's an example of a character algorithm:

Walk forward.

Collect some wood.

Algorithms must be written into a specific coding language to make the characters move. Some games require millions of steps. Those are put together by many programmers to make the characters act.

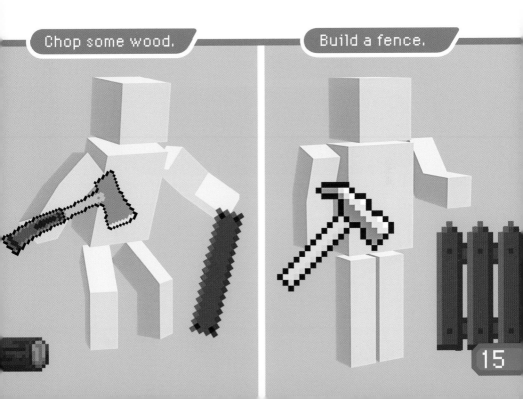

Chop some wood.

Build a fence.

Other characters besides the main character must be programmed, too. These secondary characters are programmed to do only a few different actions. They might run away, wander, or attack.

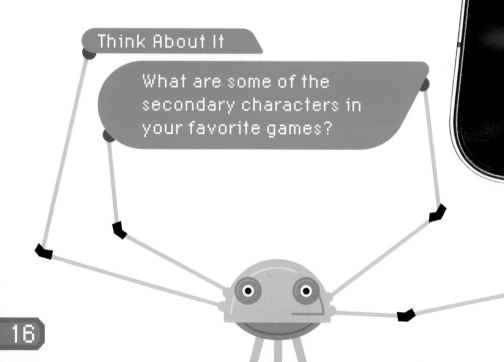

Think About It

What are some of the secondary characters in your favorite games?

ANGRY BIRDS

LOA

The green pigs are secondary characters in *Angry Birds*.

Creating a realistic video game takes more than just coding actions. Sometimes the characters need to look like real people. In that case, designers use real people as models. A model dresses in a suit with **sensors** and performs certain actions. The sensors pick up those actions and recreate them on the computer.

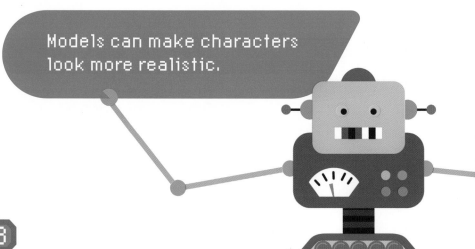

Models can make characters look more realistic.

The white balls on the suits are sensors.

Chapter 3

Watch Out!

Often in video games, enemies or obstacles pop up unexpectedly. That's part of the challenge. Programmers don't want players to be able to predict these challenges. That would get boring! When there is no pattern to the character's actions, it is called randomness.

This character doesn't know there are enemies all around!

21

Sometimes characters' choices determine what obstacles they face. A player might choose to go through obstacles to reach a goal.

Sometimes randomness has good consequences. For example, a player might get a chance to "power up."

A power-up is an object that adds to a character's life, strength, or armor.

Chapter 4

Keeping Score

Your score can go up or down in a game. The game uses **variables** to keep track of your score. Variables are also used to keep track of time played or left in a game. Variables track number of lives, too. A programmer writes the code to make the variable go up or down by one.

Sometimes programmers make mistakes, called bugs. Before a game is released, people test the game to find the bugs. Programmers fix the code so the game works properly.

Next time you play a game, think about all the work that went into its creation!

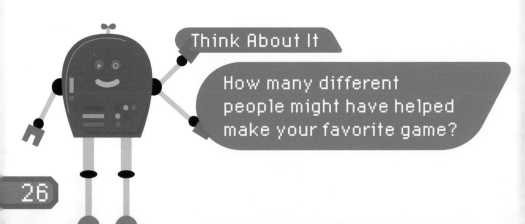

Think About It

How many different people might have helped make your favorite game?

Programmers work hard to make sure a game is the best it can be!

27

ACTING OUT AN ALGORITHM

Create your own algorithm like those used in video games.

▶ **Materials Needed:**

- A large open area you can walk across
- Several sheets of construction paper
- A goal (item) you'd like to reach, such as a stuffed animal

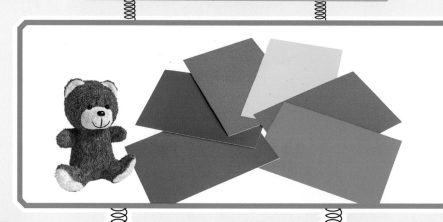

❶ Place the stuffed animal on the floor.
❷ Walk to another area of the floor. Pretend you are the character in the video game and you want to get to the stuffed animal.
❸ Lay the pieces of paper down in a pattern of your choosing on the floor.
❹ Walk the path from your starting point to the stuffed animal.

We've created one example of an algorithm for you.

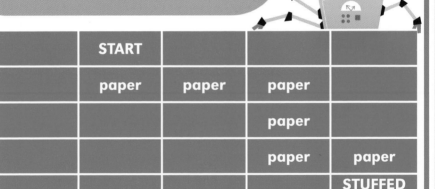

	START			
	paper	paper	paper	
			paper	
			paper	paper
				STUFFED ANIMAL

❺ What algorithm did you come up with?
❻ Try as many different algorithms as you can think of.

DEBUGGING CHALLENGE

The goal of this game is to get your character from **START** to the **GOLD COIN**. See if you can spot the mistake in the algorithm.

START

▼

▶   ▶   ▲

GOLD COIN

GLOSSARY

algorithm (al-guh-**ri**-them)
series of steps done in a certain order to do something useful

programmers (**proh**-gram-urz)
people who write programs for computers

sensors (**sen**-sorz)
devices that can detect movement and changes in heat, sound, and pressure and send the information to a computer

storyboard (**stor**-ee bord)
drawings that show the plan for the game world, characters, and action

variables (**vair**-ee-uh-buhlz)
values (such as points scored) that change as you play a game

Answer

The arrow above the gold coin should point down.

INDEX

FACTS FOR NOW

Visit this Scholastic website for more information on designing a video game: **www.factsfornow.scholastic.com**
Enter the keywords **Design a Game**

ABOUT THE AUTHOR

Marcie Flinchum Atkins teaches kids how to use computers and find the best books in her job as an elementary librarian. She holds an M.A. and an M.F.A. in children's literature and lives with her family in Virginia. Read more about Marcie at www.marcieatkins.com.